NLP DARK PSYCHOLOGY

The simple guide to start controlling the mind,

yours and anyone's

Oliver Bennet

Table of Contents

NLP DARK PSYCHOLOGY

Introduction

The NLP, which stands for Neuro-Linguistic Programming, indicates a methodology for changing the thoughts and behaviors of one or more people, to help them achieve the desired results.

Born in the 1970's in California in the middle of the New Age era, NLP owes its success with the promise (often kept) to improve work performance and achieve happiness through personal development. The founders of NLP, the psychologist Richard Bandler and the linguist John Grinder, started from the belief that they could identify successful individuals' thought patterns and behaviors and then teach them to others.

One of NLP's core techniques is constituted by imitation or, as adepts define it, modeling: by imitating the language and behaviors of successful people, it would be possible to make our skills our own and achieve their results.

NLP is mainly based on language processing and uses other communication techniques to make people change their thoughts and behaviors.

How Does It Work?

NLP is based on the idea that people operate through internal "maps" to represent the world.

Thus, NLP tries to identify these maps (which are nothing more than subjective experiences of what surrounds us) to change their orientations. It is a methodology that aims at a change of thought and behavior.

It should be specified that NLP has nothing to do with hypnosis. On the contrary, it works through the conscious use of language to modify a person's mental and behavioral patterns.

What Is It For?

NLP finds a wide field of intervention, using various techniques according to the desired purposes.

Starting from the idea that thought and behavior can be modelled, NLP is used for:

- treat anxiety, phobias and stress, thus improving emotional responses to certain situations;
- achieve successful professional goals, such as increased productivity at work and motivation;
- remove negative thoughts and feelings associated with a past event;
- improve their communication skills.

In general, NLP is used as a personal development method through the "enhancement" of one's skills, which aims to have greater self-confidence and to communicate better with others.

But What Exactly Is NLP?

NLP is a psychological method that studies people's behavior, analyses models. It thus extracts the practical techniques to teach to potentially overcome any situation (work, success, relationships).

NLP teaches that each of us can, with willpower, change and revolutionize one's life in an instant, abandoning limits through the help of concrete techniques. Each person is the architect of her destiny, determined exclusively by her decisions and not by the living conditions as many believe and which are already "prescribed" and not changeable.

NLP's message to us is the secret of living well, which is "living life trying to make the most of it". It is we, and only us, who can make everything we want possible, starting from the constancy and determination, which from the beginning must not be missing, together with the desire to fight for a purpose, therefore the energy that goes put into practice, up to the exercise, application, construction and achievement of our goal.

In a nutshell, this method would help us become the people we always wanted to be; an opportunity to learn how to use our mind and body in the most functional way possible.

Talking about NLP is equivalent to dealing with themes based on creativity, freedom, self-esteem, choices, and courage. The founders of NLP coined this term (Neuro Linguistic Programming) precisely to highlight a link between neurological processes (neuro), language (linguistics) and the various behavioral screens that have been learned only through experience (programming).

According to Bandler and Grinden, it is indeed impossible to find a field where this model cannot be applied: from self-esteem problems to sports or school skills, from courtship to success, and some even claim that this discipline somehow manages to fight depression and other psychological disorders.

Summing up, NLP has among its main purposes, the goal of developing successful habits / reactions, amplifying effective behaviors to make what we want for us to happen and decreasing unwanted ones, which limit the occurrence of our design drawings.

With Neuro Linguistic Programming, you learn to model the quality of the internal images lived and the sensations perceived to act for our benefit in the future. NLP makes us aware of our unconscious behaviors and programs that we can modify as we wish.

There are NLP academies where you can learn and put into practice all the possible techniques to achieve what you want a purpose: motivation, the basis for all our desire, is the ingredient fundamental that pushes us to fight to get it. Without it, none would be able to reach the end to which it aspires.

Optimism, joy of life and cooperation are the three secrets of living in harmony. Everyone needs a paladin.

Have you ever wished for some things for yourself and done nothing to get what you want? Have you ever wanted to let go yourself from the slavery of some addiction such as alcohol or smoking, to lose weight, to learn a language or play an instrument?

Certainly yes, but how many of you have put your goals into practice and how many people have been stuck? This is how it happens, for all those belonging to the second sphere, we finds us doing only one action: complaining. The coach then takes over and helps us take stock, find our orientation, define ourselves as people. It spurs us to find a motivation so sour "journey" becomes tortuous.

There are four types of coaches:

- Life coach: the one who helps us achieve personal goals;
- Company coach: the one who helps companies and professionals in the sector to act more effectively and with determination in professional life;

- Career coach: one who helps people in the phases of professional change, therefore a career jump or even a professional regression;
- Sport coach: helps students raise the level of performance and thus triggers mental and physical training.

Therefore, the main objective of NLP is to explain to us how everything we are is the simple result of what we have thought. Our life is in our hands.

Don't believe it? Try it for yourself!

NLP is an attitude ...

An attitude described by a sense of curiosity, adventure, and desire to learn the necessary skills to understand what communication types affect others. It is the desire to know things that are worth knowing. It is looking at life as a rare opportunity to learn.

NLP is a methodology ...

A methodology based on the principle that every behavior has a structure ... and that this structure can be extrapolated, learned, taught and even changed. The guiding criterion of this method is to know what will be useful and effective.

NLP is a technology ...

A technology that allows a person to organize information and perceptions to achieve results deemed impossible in the past.

Neuro-Linguistic Programming therefore, deals with studying the structure of subjective experience and what can be calculated from it.

The fundamental belief and promise are that effective thinking strategies can be identified, assumed and used by anyone.

NLP was born from the fruitful years of research, carried out by Richard Bandler and John Grinder, to find out what the behavioral and linguistic elements allowed successful people to have such a significant constancy of positive results.

The results were the identification of a series of specific and reproducible behavioral strategies and linguistic models.

The Hoaxes of Neuro Linguistic Programming

From psychotherapy to coaching, NLP is still lacking of substantial experimental evidence, and has many characteristics of pseudo sciences.

Neuro-Linguistic Programming (NLP) has been rejected by science in every possible and imaginable way, yet it continues to be discussed.

We can notice that in the film Kingsman - Secret service (2014), neuro linguistic programming is passed off as a seduction weapon.

It is almost impossible to find a field where the NLP, according to its supporters, cannot be applied: from courtship to leadership, from self-esteem problems to sports skills, success is at hand, and there are even those who come to propose discipline, to combat depression and other psychological disorders.

The Origins

The NLP was born in the first half of the 70s, the golden age of the New-Age, and perhaps it is no coincidence that the crib was the California lysergic. The dads in the new discipline were Richard Bandler, a psychology student at the time, and linguist John Grinder, both from the University of California, Santa Cruz, who had begun to work out a "theory of everything" of psychotherapy from their respective fields of study.

One of the foundations of the new, revolutionary branch of psychology would be imitation or, as the adepts define it, modelling: by imitating successful people's language and behavior, it would be possible to make our skills our own and achieve their results.

It is thus in fact, according to the Gospel of Neuro-Linguistic Programming, that Grinder and Bandler arrived at another fundamental intuition called Meta-model: studying the work of three famous psychotherapists and integrating it with theories by famous linguists such as Gregory Bateson and Noam Chomsky, they convinced themselves that the key to therapy was not so much what the patient said, but how he said it.

According to the NLP, three processes exist in language (generalization, cancellation and distortion) through which we unconsciously eliminate part of the information. According to the NLP, the psychotherapist's task would be to ask the patient for the words he chooses to use to understand the underlying structure. Simplifying, if the patient says, "Everyone is treating me badly" (generalization) the therapist could reply "Is there nobody who treats her well?" and so on.

Grinder and Bandler also distilled the concept of the representational system. In our mind, we create subjective representations of the reality that surrounds us based on what our senses perceive, from which derives one of the evocative mottos made by the NLP followers: "The map is not the territory". But from this reasonable (and certainly not original) premise, the fathers of the NLP arbitrarily deduced that it is possible to understand how each of us thinks, based on a series of clues from language and eye movements.

If we frequently use expressions like "I see you like cinema" we will reveal that our preferred representational system is visual. The auditory symbolic system will instead be indicated by words such as "I have heard too many speeches on this issue". Simultaneously, the kinesthetics, that is, the people who relate to reality above all in terms of touch, taste and smell, will tell us "his handshake I didn't like it." You could then use this information to experiment, experiment, other ways of processing information, or get in tune quickly.

Chapter 1:   What Is Manipulation?

 Manipulation is a social influence that works to change the habits or understanding of others, or the subject, through violent, misleading, or questionable methods. The manipulator will use to advance their interests, generally, at the expense of others, so many of their techniques would be considered deceptive, devious, violent, and exploitative.

Social influence, such as when it comes to a medical professional working to persuade their patients to start adopting healthy routines, is usually perceived to be something safe. This is true of any social impact capable of appreciating the right of those included to choose and is not unduly coercive. On the other hand, if somebody is trying to get their way and is using people against their will, the social impact can be damaging and is generally towered above.

Emotional or mental manipulation is seen as a kind of persuasion and coercion. Some parts are in this type of mind control, such as bullying and brainwashing. For such many components, individuals will see this as misleading or abusive.

Those who decide to use control will do so to manage the habits of those around them. The manipulator will have some objective in mind and will work through various abuse kinds to coerce those around them into helping the manipulator get to the last goal. Frequently, emotional blackmail will be involved.

Those who practice control will use mind control, brainwashing, or bullying techniques to get others to complete the jobs for them. The manipulator's subject may not wish to carry out the task; however, they feel that they have no other option because of the blackmail or different technique used. The majority of manipulative people has no proper caring and sensitivity towards others, so they might not see an issue with their actions.

Other manipulators just want to get to their final goal and are not concerned with who has been bothered or hurt along the way.

Also, manipulative people are typically scared to enter into a healthy relationship because they think others will decline them. Somebody who has a manipulative personality will frequently have the inability to take responsibility for their behaviors, problems, and life. Considering that they are unable to take the blame for these concerns, the manipulator will use the methods of adjustment to get another person to take control of the responsibility.

Manipulators are frequently able to use the same strategies discovered in other forms of mind control to get the impact they want over others. Among the most commonly used methods is known as emotional blackmail. This is where the manipulator will effort to inspire compassion or guilt in the subject they are manipulating. These two emotions are chosen because they are considered the two highest of all human feelings and are the most likely to stimulate others into the manipulator's action. The manipulator will then have the ability to take full benefit of the subject, using the sympathy or regret that they have developed to persuade others to comply or help them reach their final goal.

Frequently, the manipulator will not just be able to create these feelings; they will have the ability to motivate degrees of sympathy or guilt that can be an escape for the situation that is going on. This means that they can take a case such as missing out on a party, like the subject is losing out on a funeral or something more important.

Emotional blackmail is just one of the strategies that are used by manipulators. Another way that have been successful for many manipulators is to use an abuse that is called crazy-making. This technique is typically aimed at the hope of producing insecurity in the subject being manipulated; frequently, this self-doubt will.

At times, the manipulator will use types of passive-aggressive habits to bring about crazy-making. If the manipulator is trapped in the act, they will use rejection, reason, rationalization, and deceptiveness of ill intent to get out of the difficulty.

One of the most significant concerns with psychological manipulators is that they are not always able to recognize what others around them might need, and they will lose the ability to fulfill or perhaps think about these needs. This does not justify the behavior that they are doing. Still, frequently, others' requirements are not considered or are not a top priority to the manipulator, so they can perform manipulative jobs without feeling guilt or pity. This can make it hard to discuss and stop the habits in a rational way why the manipulator should stop.

Besides, the manipulator might find that it is challenging for them to form long and significant relationships and friendships because the people they are with, will always feel used and will have trouble trusting the manipulator. The problem goes both ways in the development of relationships; the manipulator will not have the ability to recognize the other individual's needs while the other person will not have the ability to form the needed emotional connections or trust with the manipulator.

Needs to Manipulate Successfully

An active manipulator should have strategies at hand that will make them effective at using people to get to their final objective. While there are different theories on what makes an active manipulator, we will look at the three needs set out by George K. Simon, a capable psychology author. According to Simon, the manipulator will need to:

1. Have the ability to conceal their aggressive behaviors and objectives from the subject.

2. Have the ability to figure out the vulnerabilities of their designated topic.

3. Have some level of ruthlessness readily available so that they will not require to deal with any doubts that may develop due to hurting the issues if it comes to that. This harm can be either psychological or physical.

The first requirement that the manipulator has to achieve:

If the manipulator goes around informing everyone their strategies or always acts mean to others, no one will stay long enough to be manipulated. Instead, the manipulator needs to have the ability to conceal their thoughts from others and act like everything is normal. By the time the subject is conscious of the concern, the manipulator has enough details to persuade the issue to continue.

Next, the manipulator will need to have the ability to determine what the vulnerabilities of their intended victim or victims are. This can help them to figure out which tactics need to be used to reach the overall goal. In some cases, the manipulator might be able to do this action through a little bit of observation while other times, they will need to have some kind of interaction with the subject before coming up with the full strategy.

The third requirement is that the manipulator needs to be ruthless.

It will not work out if the manipulator puts in all their work and then frets on how the subject will be fair at the end. It is not most likely that they would be going with this plan at all if they did care about the subject. The manipulator will not care about the subject at all and does not manage if any damage, either psychological or physical, befalls the issue as long as the general goal is fulfilled.

One reason why manipulator is so capable is that the subject often does not know they are being manipulated until later. They may believe that whatever is going on is fine; possibly, they think they have made a brand-new friend in the manipulator. By the time the subject knows they are being used or no longer wishes to be a part of the process, they are stuck. The manipulator will have the ability to use strategies, including emotional blackmail, to achieve their goal.

Chapter 2: The Manipulation Ethics: Can Be Good and Bad

Is It Possible Manipulation Could Be Good and Bad?

Mention the term 'manipulation,' and that which springs to mind is the negative connotations linked with this expression. Manipulation means deceit. Manipulation means utilizing unscrupulous and underhanded strategies to make the most of somebody else. Manipulation signifies fraud and lying. Manipulation is untrue.

The expression has got a lousy reputation through time and the words used to describe manipulation in drama paint an image that's somewhat ugly or disagreeable. "She has him enclosed around her little finger," "I advised my boss just what he wished to listen to," "He has got a reputation for being a heartbreaker," "I talked to my friend to do exactly what I desired." These typical examples of exploitation surely do not place a favorable spin on the two parties involved with the procedure. It gets the manipulator outside to be somebody who's egotistical, self-serving, misleading, and worry about having somebody else to their benefit. It earns the person who has been manipulated look absurd, clueless and perhaps even feeble of character to "allowing" themselves to be duped so easily.

Manipulation has ever been seen as an act that's callous, smart yet adorable, and consistently where one ends up being manipulated or taken advantage of. Psychotherapy is seen more negatively as it will become evident the person has heartlessly disregarded another's feelings, setting their selfish desires over everybody else. Worse is that, the manipulator has manipulated another by pretending to become their pal and then utilizing data shared in confidence.

Whether personal or professional lives, there's one fact which stays. Nobody enjoys knowing they've been manipulated. Nobody. With this kind of negativity connected with this challenging, it gets nearly impossible to feel there is a chance manipulation might be used to get an excellent, or perhaps cause change for the better.

As unexpected as it might sound, manipulation isn't all evil. Manipulation is all around us, and you often don't need to look very far to find proof of it. Take advertisers and entrepreneurs, for example, using their continuous messages telling people to purchase this, buy this, stop doing so, and quit doing this. They are all attempting to control our choices in one manner or another. Which kinds of exploitation, however, are in reality seeking to make us change for the better?

Ads that let to stop smoking and eat healthily are attempting to control our choices, and however, in this circumstance, they are trying to elicit favorable change. Stopping smoking is to your benefit. Therefore, it is eating wholesome. When it's to your good, does not that make it a right type of exploitation? Governments across the globe manipulate their people. So does faith. However, we sometimes decide to ignore it since it comes in a more "authoritative" source to speak. Businesses control their clients by producing products to improve their revenue figures and telling customers, "they can't survive without it."

Whether used for "good" or "poor," manipulation remains, after the afternoon, manipulation. Do any of us have any right to order a person's choices or activities, even when we think it's advantageous? What makes the concept of exploitation this kind of embarrassing notion to bargain with is possibly the simple fact that we do not enjoy the notion of somebody else attempting to dictate what we need to do, or even forcing us into doing anything we would not otherwise be more inclined to perform ourselves.

Managers in work attempt to control their employees all of the time, even though the fantastic leaders take action to attempt to keep their employees motivated or function at their finest. Successful supervisors have mastered the craft of favorable manipulation and flipped it into a powerful instrument used to handle their workers' performance, forcing them to achieve their objectives.

This identifying detail will be the defining distinction between what is categorized as misuse, and what is known as persuasion. Persuasion remains a kind of exploitation, but what distinguishes it in the negative standing related to exploitation boils down to 3 things:

- Your goal.
- Your honesty.
- Precisely what the advantage or positive effect will be to the person that you're attempting to convince.

These three critical points are the determining factor to know if you are trying to control or persuade. Whenever you're taking advantage of your goal, you are selfish. When you convince, it is generally well-meaning for the benefit of another individual. When you control, you lie, fool and attempt to hide what is happening. When you convince, you are competent, upfront, and honest about what you are trying to do, since you've got no reason to conceal if it is not done for personal profit. When you control, there's not any positive effect or benefit on the other party, just yourself. When you convince, another party you are attempting to influence will be the person who reaps the maximum benefit from this circumstance. Non-profit organizations hotels of persuasion attempt to get other people to behave and transform for the best way to make a positive effect on the entire world. They convince donors, increase the essential financing, and promote awareness among others concerning significant matters that have to be dealt with or altered.

Chapter 3:   Manipulation Techniques

Lying is one of the very first techniques that manipulators use. It is a technique that pathological liars or psychopaths use when they want to confuse their victims. If they are continually lying to them, their victims will often be unaware of the truth. Those who use this tactic have no moral or ethical apprehension about it.

Telling half-truths or only telling part of a story is another tactic that can be used to manipulate someone. People like this will often keep things to themselves because it puts the victim at a disadvantage. They can get what they desire by waiting to tell them the rest of the story until their needs are met.

Being around someone who has frequent mood swings can often make a person vulnerable to their manipulations. Not knowing what mood, they will be in, whether they will be happy, sad, or angry can be a beneficial tactic for the manipulator. It keeps the victim off balance and easy to manipulate because they will often do what the manipulator wants to keep them in a good mood.

Another tactic that is often used by narcissists is known as love

bombing. This doesn't automatically mean that you have to be in a relationship but it can be used in a friendship. Those that use this tactic will charm the victim to death and have them believe that this is the best relationship or company that has ever happened to them. They will use the victim for what they want, and then when they are done, they drop them and the victim has no idea of what happened.

A tactic that can be used in extreme cases by the manipulator is that of punishment. This makes the victim feel guilty for something they did wrong, even if they didn't do anything at all. Some of the disciplines that they can inflict on their victims are consistent nagging, shouting, mental abuse, giving them the silent treatment, and even as bad as physical violence.

Denial is often a tactic used when a manipulator feels pushed in a corner, and they feel like they will be exposed for the fake that they are. In this instance, they will manipulate the victim into believing that they are doing the very thing the manipulator is accused of.

Spinning the truth is a tactic often used by politicians. It is used to twist the facts to suit their needs or wants. Sociopaths use this technique to disguise their bad behavior and justify it to their victims.

Minimizing is when a manipulator will play down their behavior and actions. They move the blame onto the victim for overreacting when their actions are harmful, and the person has a valid reason for feeling the way they do.

It is often enjoyable when the manipulator pretends to become the victim. They do this to gain sympathy or compassion from their real victims. They do this so that their victims feel a sense of responsibility to help and end their suffering, especially if they feel that they are the cause of that person's suffering.

Another way that the manipulator can move the blame onto the victim is by targeting the victim and accusing them of wrongdoing. The victim will then start to defend themselves, while the manipulator hides their manipulation away from the victim. This can be dangerous because the victim is so focused on defending themselves that they forget to see what is right in front of them.

Using the positive reinforcement tactic tricks the victim into thinking that they are getting something for helping the manipulator get what they want. This can be through purchasing them expensive presents, praising them, giving them money, constantly apologizing for their behavior, giving them lots of attention and all-around buttering them up.

There are times when a person knows where they stand with someone. However, in any type of relationship, the manipulator might keep moving the goal to confuse their victim because they thought everyone was still on the same page.

Another manipulation tactic that manipulators like to use is known as diversion. This tactic is commonly used to divert a certain conversation away from what the manipulator is doing. The new topic is created to get the victim to lose focus on what the manipulator is doing or trying to do.

Sarcasm is a tactic that can lower the self-esteem and confidence of a victim through embarrassment. The manipulator will use sarcasm – usually saying something about the victim- in front of other people. This gives the manipulator power over the victim because they just made them feel very small.

Guilt trips are another tactic that a manipulator will use against their victim. In this instance, they will often tell their victims that they don't care about them or love them; they will indicate that they are selfish and that their life is easy. It keeps the victim confused and anxious because they want to please the manipulator by letting them know that they care about them and do anything for them.

Using flattery is the exact opposite of guilt-tripping. In this instance, the manipulator will use charm, praise, or other flattery types to gain the victim's trust. They victim enjoys the compliments and lets their guard down.

Another way that a manipulator will move the blame is to play the innocent card when the victim accuses them of their tactics. They will act shocked or show confusion at the accusation. The act of being surprised is convincing to the victim, and it makes them question their judgment and if what they are feeling is wrong.

A dangerous tactic that a manipulator can use is that of extreme aggression. Rage and aggression are used to force the victim to submit.

The anger and rage are a tactic that scares the victim to stop talking about the conversation. They pretty much want to help keep the manipulator's anger in check.

Isolation is another dangerous tactic used by manipulators. It is a control mechanism used by manipulators to keep their victims from their family, friends, and loved ones who can expose the manipulator for who they are. The manipulator might know that their victim can be manipulated, but their friends and family can perceive right through them, and they are not done using their victim yet.

One of the last tactics that manipulators, such as psychopaths and sociopaths use, is fake love and empathy. These people do not know how to love others besides themselves and have a hard time loving others and showing empathy towards others. They use this tactic to entangle themselves into their victims' lives to extract what they want (Learning Mind, 2012).

Remember that Dark Manipulation is a very dangerous thing and not something that anyone would want to be caught up in if they can help it. Therefore, it is important to protect yourself against anyone who would try to take advantage of you and manipulate you to get what they want. The more knowledge you have about these devious acts, the easier it is to protect yourself from it.

Chapter 4: Recognize When Someone Manipulate You

Now that we have learn about manipulation and what it is all about, it is time to take a look at how to tell when manipulation is being used against you. Many people who would love to use the power of persuasion, mind control, and more against you. This is not a bad thing all of the time. But when the manipulation is done at the expense of you and your wants, it can derail your life.

We have already consumed some time talking about how manipulation will benefit the manipulator while harming one or more victims at the same time. This is pretty scary stuff, and it is crucial we learn how to detect this manipulation to protect ourselves as much as possible. Some of the things you can do to ensure you detect manipulation when used against you include:

Watching the Behavior of the Other Person

The first thing that we like to look for is some of the behaviors that come with the manipulative person. We want to look at whether the other person talks first, if they want you to talk first, or a good combination of both. Manipulative people will like to listen to what you want to say, and they always want you to put out the information first. This is because they want to hear from you and learn what your weaknesses and strengths are over the long term. They like to ask many questions, especially ones that are about their personal life without having to answer any from you. They will seem to know a ton of information, especially personal information about you while not giving up any of their own.

Then when the manipulator does respond to you, the actions and responses will be based on any of the information they have been given. Some of the things that you should look for here include

Always wanting you to speak first is not a sign of manipulation all on its own. You should pay attention and see if there are a few other symptoms of manipulation that come into play.

The person who is doing the manipulation will not reveal a ton of personal information when they go through this conversation, but they will make sure that the focus is more on you as possible.

If you find that this behavior doesn't happen just once, but it happens regularly, it is a manipulation sign.

Although it can sometimes, come off as the person showing a genuine interest in you, remember that there will be a hidden agenda behind this questioning. If you stop for a moment and no longer answer the manipulator's questions, but instead try to ask them things, they will refuse to answer or try to change the subject if they are manipulative.

Another thing to consider here is how the person accomplishes things. If they tend to use charm, then this could be a problem. While some people will be charming, the manipulator will use this to give them something they want. This person may use charm to compliment someone before making a request. They could cook a nice dinner, ask someone for money, or help them with a project. This behavior will seem pretty harmless, but it pries you to be more willing to agree to whatever the manipulator wants.

Next, you need to look at some coercive behavior. This means that manipulators will use it to persuade someone else to do what they want, and it is often going to work with threats and some force along the way. They could threaten, criticize, and yell at the other person to get what they want.

You can also notice how the other person will handle any facts that they have. If you see that the other person likes to overwhelm you with facts or mess around with facts, this could be a sign that they are working to manipulate you a bit. Facts may be manipulated using excuses, exaggerating, withholding information, and lying. The reason why manipulator is going to do this is that it helps them to feel like they have more power in the situation than you do.

Look at the Communication

The next thing that you need to take a look at here is whether you are feeling judged or you are not good enough to the other person. This is a common technique that a manipulator is going to use. They will make sure that you can find something that you did wrong no matter how hard you try. This gives them the power, and hopefully keep you working harder to appease them. This is done by picking on them, doing sarcasm, jokes, and more.

Another tactic that the person could use is the silent treatment. This is a good one for them to gain some control. They may choose to ignore your calls, emails, text messages, and more for an unreasonable amount of time. This is done to ensure you feel some uncertainty or make you know you are punished because of something that you did. Your actions will sometimes provoke this, but often because the manipulator wants to gain some more control. And when you try to oppose them about it, they are just going to deny it, or shift the blame back on to you.

You may also notice that the manipulator uses some form of guilt trip to get what they want. This guilt trip will make you feel like you are the one responsible for the manipulator's behavior. It is also going to make it so that the victim is responsible for the happiness, success, anger, failure, and more of the manipulator. You are going to notice some things when dealing with this guilt trip from the other person, and would include:

You may see that before the guilt trip starts, there will be some phrases like "If you were more considerate, you'd" or "If you loved me, you'd."

If you find that this is causing you to agree to some things that would have never registered before, then this is a good sign that you are a victim of manipulation tactic.

And you should also take notice of whether you are regularly apologizing with the other person. This can be done when you are blamed for something that had nothing to do with you, or they make you feel responsible for the situation that you are in. For example, if you said that you would meet with the manipulator at 1, but they show up two hours late. You say that it is fine that they were late, but then they go on a guilt trip and act like the martyr saying that they never seem to do anything right ever. You end up being the wrong one and you apologize, even though they were the ones who were late in this whole case.

Chapter 5:   Dark Psychology

Dark psychology has many different elements and aspects that encompass it. While it is real that we all have these fundamentals within us to some extent, we are not all inclined to using them all the time. Most of us will use them when we feel there is no other course to take, so we get manipulative.

Ordinary people prefer not to deceive or manipulate. They will usually lean towards doing things more honestly and try their best not to hurt those around them. They will eventually go dark if they feel they were pushed into using these techniques. However, not everyone operates like this.

For various reasons that aren't always obvious, some people will dive straight into these tactics as their go-to. They can be for our good at times, but they often aren't. They will use these tricks on unsuspecting people regardless of the effects they might have on them.

You will often find that the kinds of people who actively use dark psychology techniques will usually have morals that don't match those most people might follow. These are usually people who are damaged and live their lives expressing their inner demons in toxic ways. However, some will use dark psychology because they are what can be considered cold-hearted or even evil. They usually have no regard for the wellbeing of other people whatsoever.

This will give you some insight into how these people may behave. What are few of the most common strategies you will find people using on you in situations that may have nothing to do with your work? Some of them might be used on you in your social life.

The hope is that deeper insight into these tools that have probably been used against most people, will allow them to know what to look out for and perhaps react accordingly. The other hope is that it may help people use them to change their lives for the better in various aspects of their lives, be it in their careers, education, social lives, or even their love lives.

Benign/Covert

Reverse Psychology

This is possibly one of the most popular and possibly clichéd forms of dark psychology. The main reason it can be considered benign, or non-threatening is that so many people know this method is not that difficult to spot.

However, it can be a powerful tool when used right. It is most likely to work against very stubborn people who are always likely to do the exact opposite of what they are told. With this in mind, one begins to understand why telling them to do the opposite of what you desire them to do will most likely move in the direction you want them to.

This method is also a great way to disguise your intentions and make it seem as if the target acted of their own free will.

Love Flooding

This insidious method is one of the most difficult methods to detect, especially when used subtly enough and in conjunction with reinforcement and withdrawal/denial.

Love flooding (sometimes known as love bombing) is when a predator suddenly showers a potential victim with gifts, praise and positivity. Love flooding can be dangerous because it can be used to disguise sadistic motivations behind positive actions sustained for a calculated amount of time.

How it works is that one would use this technique to have their intended victim subconsciously associate them with positive feelings. Once a

27

dependency has been established and the wanted rapport is created, it becomes easier to get the target to do as the persuader wants them to.

This method works best at the beginning of the relationship when trust is still being built.

Reinforcement

Used correctly (usually as a follow up from love flooding/bombing) this very covert tool can create an almost Pavlovian behavior in a target.

It is easy to think that the work ends when the love flooding has done its job. However there needs to be another rung on the ladder that leads to getting what one wants or interest may wane before the original desire of the persuader is met.

Restricting one's affection, attention, and praise for when someone does as the manipulator pleases creates a deep desire in the victim to do whatever it is that will make them feel good again. The target will soon behave in the required manner in order to get the positive reinforcement they believe they can get only from you.

Love Withdrawal/Denial

This step may seem a little counter-intuitive, but there is a lot of good reasoning behind using a tactic like this. It is a great follow up after love flooding/bombing and then reinforcement.

Once a person, say a potential love interest, for example, has already started associating the persuader with feelings of positivity and little reward has to be given to elicit that response, then occasionally withdrawing or denying love can be a powerful closer.

It simply creates an air of unpredictability around the manipulator while giving them complete control of their victim's mind and emotions.

This is achieved by 'randomly' giving rewards for required behavior where the reward was given every time the desired behavior was shown. It keeps the victim guessing about the manipulator's state of mind while increasingly making them crave the old attention they came to expect from them.

Passive Aggressiveness:

Guilt tripping: it is a very common way for people to avoid a confrontation to get what they want without risking an undesirable outcome.

It heavily relies on making a person feel bad by bringing up something they did, said, or even implied. It doesn't even matter if it happened. What's important is that they feel swayed by their guilt to lowering their guard enough to be nudged in the right direction.

Sarcasm: this is another tactic for getting the desired response without risking a confrontation because sarcasm is often used humorously.

Sarcasm can be used to deliver biting words funnily without giving the victim reasonable cause to flare up and get confrontational without looking like the wrong ones.

This works especially well in public areas where the one who seems to be in the wrong might call on the judgement and wrath of an on-looking crowd.

Bribery

This can take several forms and will not be as lustful as one would imagine if done right.

The trick to this is never being seen to be the one offering the bribe, but rather getting the other party to ask or even expect the bribe.

This works best if it started as simply rewarding/reinforcing good behavior so that one is never suspected of bribing, but simply cashing in on the favor they have built up over time.

It can come in the form of small gifts, money, favors, etc. It doesn't matter. What does matter is that they align with the needs of the person who is to be bribed.

This can be tricky to accomplish in the heat of the moment if favor hasn't been garnered over time, but can slowly be built up to if one is patient, compliant, and is willing to ask questions that seem innocuous while looking for the weak spot where a need can be met.

Deception:

Lying: while most people are not as good as lying as they think they are, it is not uncommon for people we meet every day to try anyway, just to be given away by their body language, if one knows where to look.

Half-truths: while these are easier to pull off, they can be trickier to remember as they can weave a story that's too difficult to navigate under pressure.

Exaggeration: blowing the truth out of proportion to some degree can be a good way to get what you desire or get out of trouble, but is difficult to get out of it if caught red-handed.

Diminishing: downplaying the truth can be just as difficult as exaggerating, but can be a good way to delay trouble while looking for an escape route.

Omission: leaving out facts in a story is easily a favorite of many persuaders as the blame can be placed on the victim if anything goes wrong.

Fraud: this is the drawn-up act of creating an elaborate scheme to get one's way, but the consequences of it can far outweigh the good, in most cases.

Implication: this entails using certain words just to claim one may have a different understanding of those words if questioned later. It offers plausible deniability.

Yes-stacking

'Yes-stacking' is simply asking someone a series of questions they are most likely to answer yes to. Once they have done this more than three times in a row, it becomes easier to ask them for what you like as most humans feel a strong need to seem congruent with themselves. So if

someone suddenly answers 'no' after having answered in the affirmative so many times they can end up answering yes just to avoid the discomfort of feeling, or even seeming incongruent with themselves.

Slightly harder cases can often be leaned on with a bit of guilt by reminding them of their own words and this will further trigger their innate need to seem congruent to themselves and others. Yes-stacking is often used by many people in the sales industry to 'close' the sale with a customer.

Subliminal Influence:

Visual: this is the method of using images, often subtly, to get certain ideas into someone's mind without them suspecting that they are being manipulated.

Carefully placing an object, color, or image that triggers certain feelings where they'll be visible without being obvious will ingrain those feelings in a deeply subconscious way. This can be seen anywhere from presidents (and presidential candidates) wearing specifically colored neckties, to an everyday person placing an object with a certain picture in the background of a video chat because one knows that it will subconsciously bring those feelings to the surface.

Audio: using this can be trickier to use on an individual, but can be very powerful to get them to do what one wants without their knowledge. Examples of this can be in Hollywood horror movies where the sound is used to set up a 'jump-scare'. The sounds themselves can create such an intense atmosphere that nothing scary has to happen on the screen for people to jump out of their seats. Marketers with memorable jingles in their adverts can use this to get people to think about their products long after the ad is over.

Chapter 6: What is NLP?

NLP is short for neuro-linguistic programming. The term neuro refers to one's nervous system, while linguistic refers to language control. Neuro-linguistic programming is a form of conscious programming used to control neural languages or, in layman's terms, a translator and controller into how your brain thinks.

Why is NLP a thing? Well, it's pretty hard to communicate when you don't speak the language. Now imagine you want to go to a K-pop concert in South Korea. To go, you will have to get the ticket and find the venue and then stand in line and get in. Now imagine any of those three things get lost in translation, either you end up at the wrong ticket site because you don't understand the language or have the tickets. Still, you end up at the wrong venue because you went to the Hong riverfront instead of the Hang riverfront. How about you did all that but got thrown out of the concert venue because you tried to rush through the doors when it clearly said that particular entrance wasn't for fans?

One tiny mess up and your entire experience is ruined. Even just thinking about it makes you want to scream, doesn't it?

Now, imagine how that relationship works in terms of your mind.

Your conscious mind and subconscious mind are like two identical twin brothers separated at birth and raised in two different countries. They may have the identical genetic makeup, but it makes next to no sense when they talk to each other because they don't speak each other's language.

Why Is This A Problem?

Because the two brothers have to work together!

Now imagine your conscious mind plans to get fit and healthy. You have decided that as of today, you will be eating well, cut out sugars and all those processed trans fats, and top it all off you are also going to hit the gym and start working on your body. You've made up your mind, gone out and bought everything you need, written everything down, told everyone not to call you and randomly order pizza—you've done everything you need to do, except let your subconscious brain know.

Now, this is a problem, because while your conscious brain is your goal setter and the main decision maker when it comes to what you are going to do and what you aren't going to do, your subconscious brain plays an equally important role, as a goal getter. Your subconscious brain is the facilitator, it's the engineer that made the Apple products so good that Steve Jobs could go out and be Steve Jobs.

Your subconscious brain is like the procurement officer of a major supermarket. While your consciousness is out there being the salesman convincing everyone to shop here, your subconscious is getting you all the products and produce you need to ensure that your consciousness has something to sell.

NLP is your bridge. It not only makes sure your conscious brain receives clear instructions, but it also has those instructions translated so that your subconscious brain can implement it! How great is that!

How Common is NLP?

But hold up! What if NLP is so easy to use, is everyone using it?

Well, to be honest, there is no way to tell.

They could be, although it's unlikely that every single person around you is employing NLP on you, that doesn't mean it can't happen!

What you're trying to ask here, though, doesn't have a lot to do with NLP being all the rave or being the social outcast. You're trying to figure out how likely you are to be exposed to NLP and if you will be controlled by it.

No, we're not using NLP on you right now, we're not reading your mind either—it's just simple deduction.

What you should do, though, is get rid of this unnecessary fear. If you are scared of something, and it is weighing on your mind to the extent where you are forcing yourself to ask indirect questions to sum it out, you need to face it head-on.

Does being manipulated scare you?

Do you think the form of mind control you are most likely to face is NLP? Don't cower and pretend it's not a problem when you think it is, if it's NLP you are scared of, deal with it.

Learn it, and arm yourself against its application.

Remember, your fears and problems are only as big as you make them out to be. Meaning if you think NLP is a treat, all you have to do is neutralize it.

Chapter 7:   NLP Techniques

NLP techniques have proved useful in many situations. It is also a fascinating subject from a psychological perspective.

One of its main aims is to link our neurological functions and language with how we behave through experience. In other words, we can gradually begin to develop more flexible behaviors by correcting our cognitive representations and reducing the importance we attach to fixed mental maps.

NLP is an interesting and useful way of changing our reality and shaping our minds to see the world more freely, more positively, and happily.

1- Separation Technique

Neuro-linguistic programming, anxiety, and stress, such as lack of confidence, are some activities and processes, not permanent situations. So, it is necessary to control these processes and change them to work for us, not against us.

One way to accomplish this is by the separation technique. The steps of this technique are as follows:

Identify the feeling you no longer want to feel and remove it from your mind. This can be many things from nervous, sadness, fear, and frustration.

Focus on the particular feeling or situation that usually makes you feel that way. For example, I get angry every time I find out my colleague is talking behind my back.

Activate that scene as if you were in a movie. Then put a fun soundtrack in the background that will make it less of a drama. Then, play this scene several times to reduce the negative feeling. This way, you will feel that things are under your control and this is not important. It may even seem funny to you now. Your anger must have dis.. this.

2- Redirection

The second thing about the neuro-linguistic programming techniques is that we don't use or don't use it correctly, no matter how obvious. If you think obsessively those bad things will happen and the worst possibility of everything, you can cause something bad to happen to you.

For example, some people can't stop thinking about what will happen if their spouse leaves them. So much so they develop obsessive behaviors that include jealousy, insecurity, and many destructive emotions. Then their biggest fears come true: they leave their wives because they can't stand them.

One of the NLP techniques is changing its meaning. It is a cognitive technique that takes our attention from fear and redirects it towards more constructive things.

For example, you should stop focusing on the fear of losing your partner and spend quality time with him.

You can turn your fear of being alone into accepting your responsibilities. So you learn to love yourself enough and learn to be strong rather than stuck with fears.

3- Neuro-Linguistic Programming: Hoeing Technique

Hoeing technique is a classic NLP technique for personal growth. What about the anchor? The anchor is the link between stimulus and emotion. The aim is to achieve more appropriate, but powerful thinking. This will make you more successful in what you need to do later.

Think about situations that make you worry or feel insecure: exams, public speaking, approaching someone you like, etc. If you succeed in being in the right mood, you get the motivation and self-esteem to get rid of worrying about these situations as if you were pulling the butter out. Here are a few steps to apply the hoeing technique by NLP principles:

First, decide how you want to feel: confident, happy, calm...

Then try to remember a time when you had these intense feelings.

Focus on this moment and take a picture of it in your mind.

Now, to apply the hoeing technique, choose a sentence of your own: "I am peaceful" or "Everything will be fine."

You must repeat this sentence until it is integrated with your mind (a desired emotion, memory, visual, anchor word). This will automatically happen whenever you need it.

Manipulate the Mind through NLP

How does the mind of a successful and happy person work? What is the key to your triumphs? What is it that makes you so productive? Could their patterns be copied so anyone could also succeed in everything that was proposed? These are queries that were asked, in the mid-70s, by the mathematician, computer expert and Gestalt therapy student, Richard Bandler, and the linguist John Grinder at the University of California (Santa Cruz, USA).

To find answers, they spent several years filming, observing, analyzing and modeling great communicators of the time, extraordinary people who excelled in their profession, in the sciences, in the arts, and business. At the beginning of this study, they focused their research on understanding how, through communication and language, changes in people's behavior occurred. To do this, they took as models three famous psychotherapists, Fritz Perls, creator of Gestalt therapy, Virginia Satir, family therapist, and Milton Erickson, a hypnosis specialist and one of the most recognized psychiatrists of our time. Through this search, they identified and codified the verbal and behavioral patterns these privileged heads used systematically and spontaneously in communicating with their patients. That was the basis of the effectiveness and success of their work.

NLP has continued to evolve. Today, it is used with great success in psychotherapy, health, sales, business, leadership, public speaking, negotiation, education, sports training, and assertive communication, among other fields. Indeed, as the psychologist, Frank Pucelik, a collaborator who worked with Bandler and Grinder in the early years of the study says, "NLP can be applied to everything in the head to do something used. Anything that being human builds, learns, or creates is a mirror of how the mind works. If your mind works better, the things you do will be better."

NLP has revolutionized the world of personal development, and not only gives us the keys to deciphering how our mind works, but with the practice of its simple and powerful tools everyone "can generate new behaviors in any area of their lives and modify unwanted behaviors (habits, fears, phobias, traumas...) Solve self-esteem problems, and communication such as difficulties to speak in public, shyness, better understand or understand what they say. The attainment of its objectives and purposes in any other field," says Gustavo Bertoloto, who introduced NLP's teaching in Spain, and author of Activate your potential with NLP in 1989.

How can a person be good at something? Judith Delozier, a participant in the original group of students of John Grinder and Richard Bandler, gives us the answer: "With practice, practice and more practice, and is that the continued practice develops an understanding and mastery of the structure that allows us to do. We become familiar with the underlying strategy, that is, with the series of events (attitudes and actions) that sustain our success, if we become aware of what the beliefs, values , and actions that form the basis of our success are, we can reproduce it and perhaps apply it in other contexts in which we want equally successful results.

For example, the most efficient people have a map of the world that allows them to perceive as many options and perspectives as possible. They have a road map, an open mind."

Techu Arranz adds: "The most effective people are those who have beliefs, internal dialogue and imagination that work in their favor, enhancing their resources and generating a state of happiness and confidence." Throughout our lives, we have all been programming vital strategies that were useful at a given moment, but after their positive intention has expired, they may be limiting us. NLP techniques make it possible to deactivate many of these limiting programs simply and enjoyably, in a curious journey that offers you a possibility of redecorating your life and re-map your map.

Chapter 8:   Using NLP To Manage People: Verbal and Nonverbal

When it comes to managing people effectively, it's important that you first understand the non-verbal cues they provide, to be able to apply your skills toward influencing them. This is an important principle in applying the NLP technique. Following are a few NLP techniques that can allow you to influence people's perception and thinking:

Deciphering Eye Movements

It is essential to understand the meaning of eye movements because each eye movement tells its tale. For instance, when searching for the right word, or trying to remember a name, you automatically move your eyes in a certain way (most likely, squinting). Rolling the eyes signals contempt, or exasperation.

Winking indicates flirtation, or a joke.

Widening the eyes signals surprise, or shock; even extreme excitement. Eye movements are also implicated in other facial expressions.

The eyes can reveal much more about people's mental and emotional status, all on their own.

Once you understand what other people's thought processes are, you can accurately follow a course of action or dialogue which acknowledges the unspoken response, as signaled by the eyes. And as you may know, eye movements complement other communication forms such as hand movements, speech, and facial expressions.

Dilation of the pupils, breathing, angle of the body, and the hands' position – all these are complementary to the spoken message. Still, eye movement is very important in communication, because every movement is influenced by particular senses and the different parts of the brain.

Here is how you can generally interpret eye movement:

Visual Responsiveness

- Eyes upward, then towards the right:

Whenever a person tilts eyes upward and then to the right, it means that the person is formulating a mental picture.

- Eyes upward, then towards the left:

Whenever a person tilts eyes upward, followed by an eye movement to the left, it means the person is recalling a certain image.

- Eyes looking straight ahead:

Whenever someone focuses directly in front of them, as though looking at a point in the distance, this indicates that they are not focused on anything in particular. That is the look often referred to as 'glazed'.

Auditory Responsiveness

- Eyes looking towards the right:

When a person's eyes shift straight towards the right, it means the person is constructing a sound.

- Eyes looking towards the left:

When a person's eyes shift straight towards the left, it indicates that the person is recalling a sound.

Audio-digital responsiveness

• Eyes looking downward, then switching to the left:

When someone drops their eyes and then proceeds to turn their eyes to the left, this signals that the person is engaged in internal dialogue.

• Eyes looking right down then left to right:

When a person looks downward and then proceeds to turn their eyes to the left and then, to the right in consecutive movements, it means the person is engaged in negative self-talk.

Kinesthetic Responsiveness

Here, the person looks directly down, only to turn the eyes to the right. That is an indication that the person is evaluating emotional status. This further indicates that the person is not at ease.

Verbal Responses

Rhythmic Speech

The idea here is not to be poetic as you speak, but to speak regularly. The recommended pace of speaking is equated to the heartbeat, say, between 45 and 72 beats per minute. At that pace, you are likely to sustain the listener's attention and establish greater receptivity to what you're saying. While normal conversational speed averages about 140 words per minute, slowing down a little and taking time to pause is highly effective to sustain people's attention. Your regular cadence should be punctuated by fluctuations in tone and emphasis not to sound monotonous.

Repeating Key Words

When you are trying to influence someone, there are key words or phrases that carry additional weight as far as your message is concerned. This speaking method is a way of embedding the message in the listener and subtly suggesting that your message is valid and worthy of reception. Repeating key words also suggests commitment, conviction and mastery of the subject matter.

Using Strongly Suggestive Language

Use a supportive and positive language of what you are saying, using a selection set of strong, descriptive words or phrases. As you do this, you should observe the person you are speaking to closely, in a manner that makes them feel as though you are seeing right through them and aware of what they are thinking. Don't be invasive about this, or aggressive.

Merely suggest that you have a keen appreciation of what makes people tick by way of your gaze. This places you in a dominant position, especially when accompanied by dominant body language, like "steepling". It helps to use suitable, complementary body language as you speak, to underscore the message subtly.

Touching The Person Lightly, As You Speak

Touching the person as you speak to them draws their attention to you in a relaxed and familiar way. By employing this technique, you're preparing the listener to absorb what you are saying to them and programming attentiveness. Those engaging in inter-gender conversations in the workplace should take great care with this technique, as it can lead to misunderstandings.

Using A Mixture Of "Hot" And "Vague" Words

"Hot" words are those that tend to provoke specific sensations in the listener. When you use them to influence someone's thinking, it is advisable to use them in a suitable pattern. Examples of phrases containing hot words are: feel free; see this; because; hear this. The effect of employing these words and phrases is that you're directing influencing the listener's state of mind, including how they feel, imagine, and perceive. You're also appealing to the sense most prevalent in the listener's conscious style (as observed through the movement of their eyes).

For example, the phrase "hear this" will appeal to those who indicate a tendency to respond most actively to auditory stimuli.

Using The Interspersal Technique

The interspersal technique is the practice of stating one thing while hoping to impress something entirely different on the listener. For example, you could make a positive statement like:

John is very generous, but some people take advantage of him and treat him as gullible.

When someone hears this statement, the likely assumption is that you want people to appreciate John's generosity. That is likely to be the message heard and yet, the subtext is that while John is generous, he is also

considered gullible and thus, at a disadvantage in life, when it comes to other people. Your hidden agenda may be to influence the listener to think of John as gullible, which calls into question his judgment. So, emphasize the words "but" and "gullible". The word "but" serves to transition the perceived compliment to John to an implicit slight.

The techniques just described form strategies in the service of influencing people. They're not intended to force a viewpoint, or to control people's behavior for nefarious ends. These techniques are intended to modify undesirable behaviors, resulting in workplace difficulties, including the failure of staff to work well together, or to complete team projects. They're also extremely helpful in the context of relationships with young people and children, whether at home, or in a learning environment.

Techniques of subtle manipulative effect like those described, though capable of influencing people and their behavior, don't amount to anything even approaching coercion. The person being spoken to chooses all responses and is merely influenced, or steered toward those responses.

Chapter 9:   Persuasion

What Is Persuasion?

What comes to your mind when you think about this question? Some think it is creating a desperate message to buy a product, while others think it tries to influence voters. The problem is a powerful force in everyday life, which has a major impact on security. Policies, legal decisions, media, news, and insights are all influenced by decisions' power and influence us. At times, we want to believe that we are not affected by persuasion. We have the natural ability to look at this sale, recognize the situation's truth, and make our own decisions. This may be true in some scenarios, but it is not necessarily the seller trying to convince you, or a TV commercial asking you to buy the latest and greatest item. Persuasion can be subtle, and there can be many factors in how we try to gain influence.

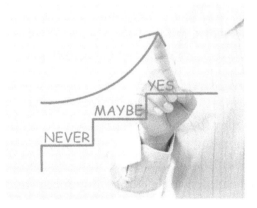

According to Perloff (2003), influence can be defined as a symbolic process in which communicators try to persuade other people to change their perspectives or behaviors regarding an issue through the transmission of a message in an atmosphere of free choice.

The Main Reasons for this Definition are:

- It is recommended to use words, photos, sounds, etc.

- This is an explanation to influence others.
- Persuasion is useful. No one found the choice is yours.
- How to provide a particular action in different cases, including verbal, unnecessary, dissemination, and information.

How Is It Different Today?

Art and the method we chose accurately determined the ancient Grecques' times, but there are significant differences shown in the past. In his book "The Dynamics of Belief: Communication and Attitudes in the 21st Century, Richard M. Perlov describes the five most important questions that new questions are different from others.

The number of persuasive measures has increased significantly. For a moment, think about how many you can find each day. To ensure the number of times the US results are reached, it ranges from about 300 to over 3,000. Make sure the communication is quick. This is the reason, and the intent to spread it very quick. Persuasion is a business that is followed by companies (distributors, companies, public companies, etc.) that only operate for a specific purpose.

Persuasion is not trivial. Of course, few ads use very compelling strategies, but many messages are much more subtle. For example, a particular schedule may be set very precisely to plan for product purchase or life extension. The question is more complicated. As customers are more identifiable and make more decisions, they need to determine when they can persuade compelling media and messages.

Modern Persuasion:

Pratkans & Aron (1991) states that some companies make better decision than others. In contrast to the means of communication that control transactions, the right decisions are left to the advertisers. Discussions are raised in response to the authority, not by or in the power of the administration. Rules are chosen based on their ability, not the royal family, but one of the biggest reasons. Good looking and behaving candidates almost always win.

The old Greeks had a better approach to making decisions. The Greeks, who are stationed, can hire an employee to protect him. The hiking teachers and writers probably decided to know-you can say they were the best students in the world. Sophists argued that a persuasion is a tool that helps find the truth. They thought that the discussion and the reason for the debate would generate good ideas and allow good ideas to come back. It did not matter what problem he was working on. Sophists would have been in the middle of discussions for some time. The stated goals of them have been confirmed that the truth has been resolved. They believed in the free practice of good ideas.

Does it sound like our world? No, we are leveraging success, and we can state that this is more than an opportunity did. But what is the modern approach to answering the question of whether it is right or wrong? Of course. It is important to reach the masses "through the manipulation of symbols and most of us human emotions." to achieve their goals, I think that subject is taught at school because the ability to ask and examine questions is directly related to someone's success in life. I think they know the right tactics as much as they know the letters of the alphabet and the right way, or how to improve CPR.

But how can we reflect the ten principles of belief? How many of us can find the situation and the right tool for the job? How many people know the times when someone is influenced by someone every day? Do this: Take a look at your decision, or your pantry, or your organization. Everyone you see is a trophy that represents some of the companies that exceed their goals. For some reason, or perhaps no reason at all, they may allow you to make your money on your products. Many influencing factors play a role in our security. They are at the top of your business and thrive by letting you think, do what you want, and get it done.

Most people are unaware of these effects or, if they are, overestimate the amount of freedom needed to realize their thoughts. But we know that a strong influence is a question that will help your decision to determine his approach if he can handle the situation and choose the right approach.

Methods of Persuasion:

The ultimate goal of persuasion is to persuade one to internalize the right argument and adopt that new attitude as part of the decision. Below are just a few of the most effective ways to persuade. Other methods include rewards, positive or negative experiences, and many other uses.

Create your Needs:

One way of identifying is to create the needs you really need. This kind of exam is a fundamental pre-requisite for whether it is a matter of self-determination and self-realization. Manufacturers often use this method to solve problems. For example, think about how many suggestions you need to find a particular product and make sure it is good.

Addressing Social Needs:

It is another very effective method that appeals to the need to be popular, and renowned. Television ads provide many examples of these types of questions. It is essential to buy these questions to look like a known or familiar person. Television is a big challenge to convince people.

Use Old Words and Photos:

It is also widely used for using loaded words and images. Advocates will notice the power of positive words that frequently use phrases such as "new and improved" or "all-natural."

Put Your Foot in the Door:

Another reason why it is ineffective to get people to meet their requirements is known as the "get it started" technique. This means that it is important to ask a question to answer a small question, such as asking a small question to be answered by creating the query. By having a person accept the first favor, the applicant is more likely to "feel," and that person is more likely to agree with the more extensive requirements. For example, a neighbor has asked you to babysit two children for one or two. If you agree, ask if you can ask your child for the rest of the time.

You have always chosen smaller requirements, so you might feel the obligation to face larger ones. This is an excellent example of what applies to approval rules, and we recommend that you use this method to encourage consumers to buy your product.

Increase and then Decrease:

This approach is different from the foot-in-the-door approach. Specific questions often start with making unnecessary requests. A person responds by rejecting the door for sale and figuratively blaming it. The answer to this question is to create a much smaller requirement that is often considered invalid. Feel the obligation to meet these offers. Since they rejected this initial request, they often help answer small requests.

Harness the Power of Security:

When you have someone in you, it can be overwhelming to bring your family back kindly. It is known as a kind of correctness. Someone did something for you, so a particular obligation to do something for someone. Manufacturers can use this method as if they were giving kindness, including "extras" and making decisions to force offers or purchases of offers.

Create another Point for Innovation:

Decisions are subtle cognitive biases that can impact diet and decisions. If you try to reach a decision, the first offer tends to decide for all future decisions. Therefore, if you try to propose a number first and try to negotiate for a particular question, it can affect future negotiations in your life, especially if the number is a little higher. This first number is the correct point. You may not get it, but a high start can lead to higher offers from your employer.

Limit Availability:

Robert Cardin's decision is known for six principles that influence the fact that it is best explained in his strongest influence in 1984 on influence. One of the keys he identified is known to be secure or to limit the availability of something.

He suggested that situations improve when things are scared or limited. We would buy something if they believed it was the last one or it would be there soon. For example, the answer could only be a limited run of a particular print. Only some printouts are available, so you may decide before you leave.

Spend Time Realizing that you have a Question:

Examples are just a few of the main persuasion techniques described by certain psychologists. Look for persuasive examples in your daily life. An interesting experiment is to revisit the 30 minutes of a particular schedule and write down a compelling assessment of all kinds. With a certain number of techniques used in a short time, you may be surprised.

Chapter 10: Principles of Persuasion

In general, persuasion can be understood as a form of strategic communication that has the purpose of convincing others. Through persuasion, it is possible to cause someone to assume a particular position, perform a specific task or accept an idea.

This communication incorporates an adequate posture, emotional appeals and, mainly, a strong and logical argumentation. In this manner, you will see that the psychology of persuasion is associated with some basic topics such as knowledge, rhetoric, and image.

This competence is important for everyone, regardless of profession or branch of activity. Still, it becomes even more indispensable for leadership positions, sales professionals, and those who work on projects, among others. And, like most behavioral skills, it can be assimilated and perfected.

The Psychology of Persuasion

In the book The Psychology of Persuasion, author Robert Cialdini states that the individual can develop this ability to communicate to persuade others' actions and decisions. Based on his studies, Robert Cialdini created the persuasive communication theory, which is based on the concept of taking advantage of some collectively internalized patterns of behavior to suggest behaviors. As stated above, this theory lists the 6 principles of the psychology of persuasion, which can be taught, learned, and applied. They are:

Reciprocity

This principle of persuasion defines that people are more willing to agree to a request when they have received something in return. Social norms urge us to respond positively to those who have done us a favor or helped us at some other time.

Consistency

The individual is also more likely to follow a pattern if he finds that this model is consistent with his ideals and values.

Authority

According to this principle, the seniority and authority transmitted by the communicator are determining aspects for others to feel liable to approve or validate something. At this point, the argument and posture of the communicator have special emphasis.

Social Validation

According to Cialdini, the greater the common sense about a behavior, the greater the probability of adopting attitudes that fit this standard.

Shortage

In this principle, the author reiterates that the charm generated by a product, service or situation is inversely proportional to its availability. That is, the more scarce, the more relevant.

Friendship / Sympathy

Finally, the sixth principle indicates that people are more inclined to collaborate or form an agreement with others when they identify with them, have a friendly relationship or some kind of attraction.

It is worth remembering that the principles of Robert Cialdini's influence should not be used in an autonomous manner but in a combined way as part of more efficient and provocative communication.

The Importance of Empathy

It is worth emphasizing that the power of persuasion can only be perfected through an additional ability: to listen with the sincere intention of understanding the other. Thus, the issuer's speech deserves full attention. It is necessary to understand the message and the lines between and everything behind each comment, such as concerns, expectations, and feelings.

For this, it is essential to be prepared to listen and at the same time collect information, emotions, and impressions. It is important to emphasize that knowing how to listen encompasses rational and emotional aspects, but does not imply an agreement with the other. Disagreements can remain, but with effective communication, they become better understood.

The Strength of Argumentation

The argumentation, in turn, is based on coherence and uses real facts to consolidate a thesis. A good argument is filled with examples, data, technical studies, research, and comparisons, to prove the integrity of an affirmation or the feasibility of a proposal. Thus, the communicator manages to involve others, causing everyone to follow the same reasoning line until they are persuaded.

This power of persuasion is appreciably amplified when argumentation joins empathy. In this case, you will be able to create a communication that mixes reason and emotion, reaching the main centers of the conviction.

Persuasion in The Corporate Universe

It is now easy to see that relationships have become increasingly virtual and often less productive. This movement is caused not only by the advancement of technology but also by the underutilization of important skills.

Among these skills are empathy and the ability to argue, which can ensure healthier and more collaborative relationships, especially in the corporate environment - where peaceful coexistence between professionals with the most diverse profiles is a basic need.

Individualism has become a major problem, hampering teamwork and collectivity. That's why you need to be careful about the virtualization of communication and the almost exclusive use of e-mail, messaging applications, and social networks.

It is also important to consider that dialogue is one of the most efficient ways to perceive fears, motives, and needs, normally hidden in fully digital communication. Personal contact creates ideal conditions for feedback, negotiation, guidance, counseling, and persuasion.

Besides, the correct application of the psychology of persuasion is one of the main characteristics of true leaders who can inspire and engage their teams. Therefore, this subject must be present in the leadership development program. With powerful argumentation, it is possible to induce critical thinking - a key ingredient in forming high-performance teams. The results will be even better if the communicator is recognized as a positive reference that inspires others.

Aspects That Impact The Power Of Persuasion

Some simple aspects can impact the persuasive power of the individual. Therefore, attention should be paid to the following tips:

Posture, Gesture, and Tone of Voice

Posture, gestures, and tone of voice are points that generate trust and credibility. Thus, it is necessary to perceive these characteristics and to conform to the model imposed by its interlocutor. Eye contact is part of this same tactic because it ensures greater proximity. With a few attempts, a connection arises.

Language

The language should also be appropriate to the model of the interlocutor so that the conversation flows naturally. It is also important to reach the emotions of the people through stimuli aligned with personal yearnings and goals. These are excellent ways to persuade.

Interruptions

To be persuasive, avoiding interruptions is essential. Cuts and hasty conclusions are signs of anxiety and unpreparedness. A productive dialogue demands time, tranquility, and attention.

Convergent Questions

Questions help the communicator keep the conversation focused on his or her primary goal. This attitude contributes to a more dynamic conversation because, through structured questions, the interlocutor is also invited to rethink his opinions and evaluate new alternatives.

Knowledge

A sound argument depends on knowledge. Therefore, it is essential to be updated, have clear answers, understand the events, interpret data, and establish communication strategies.

The psychology of persuasion principles are important skills that can be gained through specific training, discipline, and focus. Adjustments in one's behavior are fundamental in this process of improvement, which will reward one to achieve more productive interpersonal relationships - indispensable for a successful career.

Chapter 11:   NLP Techniques for Persuasion

Here's a couple of useful techniques that can help persuade someone.

1. Start a Conversation

Firstly, initiate your conversation on the correct path. This technique requires that the persuader make sure that the individual is familiar with the topic. Next is to be very clear and straightforward in what you say. Saying that "Anna failed" is a very unclear statement. Did you mean to indicate that Anna failed in her exams, an interview, or a quest? When you put forward a statement that can be misinterpreted, you need to use the correct vocabulary to explain it.

2. Pulsate the Person

The next thing is to know what pulsates the individual. Trying to get permission from your principal to organize a night party, you need to know what pulsates your principal. If your principal is someone who feels good when he is appreciated and praised, you can praise him as much as possible to get the permission. Give the individual a brief idea about the bigger picture in your words.

3. Build Rapport

Next is to build rapport while staying humble. If you are skilled enough to build rapport, then you are entitled to a pass to their trust. A successful persuasion starts with a good rapport based on the trust the individual harbors towards the persuader.

4. Remain Calm, Composed and Humble

Staying humble, without seeming to compete with the individual and not making them feel that you think you are better than them, is critical during the persuasion process. Sending that sort of message will usually only cause the individual to stick strongly to his point, making it hard for you to persuade.

5. Absorb and Concentrate

Instead of figuring out what should be said next, absorb and concentrate on the individual's being said. Now, this is a pretty hard task; this develops gradually as you go along the way. When you pay enough attention to what the individual says, you will be able to reply to him properly. Still, if you were only thinking of what to say next, you might go off topic, indicating your inattention and leading to a poor discussion. When the person is talking, make sure that you don't interrupt their statement just because you got the point; if that happens, the person might forget his point and get stressed about it.

6. Keep Track and Target a Suitable Time

One of the most important factors to consider when staring the persuasion process is time. If the person does not have adequate time to discuss with you, then whatever you have to say might be not considered due to the lack of time they possess. Therefore, before initiating the conversation, you need to ask if the individual has enough time for a talk.

7. Be Respectful and Do Not Judge

Don't judge or disrespect anything that the individual says; you need to empathize with what that individual says without giving him direct opposing comments or replies. You need to be well aware of the language that you use so that the other person does not get offended. Sometimes during the discussion, you might get emotional, which can make the process like an argument, indicating an unhealthy persuasion process.

Advantages of NLP

These NLP techniques can increase the level of influence that you exert on others. Companies that engage in marketing and sales completely depend on persuading their customers or clients to buy their products; the strategies presented in NLP guide these sellers and dealers to increase the chance of influencing their customers in making decisions. NLP also increases the person's performances; NLP helps you modify and replace your negative behaviors with more positive ones. These strategies also help you to improve your leadership style. Being humble and non-judgmental allows you to have a better communication style, even outside the persuasion process.

Essentials for Persuasion

1. Empathy – this is an essential quality that a persuader requires. You should not only be thinking about yourself, but you also should try to put yourself in the other person's shoes and think about how they might be feeling. Empathy also helps deter you from being judgmental.

2. Listening Skills – only a good listener will persuade another person; a person who is always ready for an argument will never be a good listener. If you want to be a positive and good persuader, you need to listen to what the other individual says and pay attention to their body language.

3. Indirect and Clever Commands – people tend to be more responsive to suggestions than questions. For example, instead of using the words

"Would you like to go to the concert?", you can say "Come, let's go to the concert"; this motivates a more positive response.

4. Restrict The Choices That You Provide – try not to allow the individual to say "No" or make it as hard as possible for the individual to say "No." Taking the same example, instead of asking, "Will you be able to stay long at the concert?", ask them, "Would you like to stay here for three hours or four?". The latter question makes it hard for the individual to say a "No."

5. Allow the Person to Visualize – successful persuaders always help the client or the individual visualize so that they can convince them. An example would be, "this concert will make us scream the lyrics of our favorite songs."

6. Always Make It Simple as Possible – trying to convince the other person by bragging will only be a failure; keep it as simple as possible and remember you should never put their views down.

Chapter 12: Gaslighting

We would like to go over several reality denial techniques that have been grouped under the term 'Gas lighting.' This particular form of manipulation can be quite insidious and difficult to protect yourself from. We can still introduce you to some common methods and suggest to you some possible means of defense to combat this dark art.

Gas lighting is popularly used by the Dark Triad, most commonly in the following ways:

·   Machiavellians - Machiavellians will typically employ Gas lighting to protect a particular self-image that they would like to portray. On Internet forums or social media such as Facebook, this most commonly includes taking arguments out of context or looking for an argument's weakest aspect to attack the other person's credibility. They often spend a lot of time in political forums as this is an emotional subject for many and therefore an easy place to get themselves the attention they crave. Typically, they offer a broad subject, a vague solution (or no solution), and then let people start arguing. It's trolling, but trolling in the sense that the Machiavellian is doing it to forward a self-image of appearing calm and rational to cultivate their self-image at the expense of the unsuspecting.

·   Psychotics - Psychotic motives are much harder to place, but typically they involve self-advancement. A psychotic might seem cheerful and kind at work, for instance, and yet if they are competing with another for a promotion, they will spend a lot of their free time deciding how they can discredit the other. They will not hesitate to magnify the details of a situation to get a co-worker fired if they are in their way. This lack of remorse and empathy is what makes this member of the Dark Triad so deadly. They are easily the worst of the group.

·   Narcissists - Narcissists will typically employ Gas lighting to attack anyone they feel is arguing with them. The goal is to debilitate the individual in the eyes of others; thus, elevating the Narcissist status. It may also be used as simple punishment for someone who has dared to challenge their precious self-image.

So, how do you recognize when someone is attempting to use Gas lighting techniques to disorient you or to undermine your confidence? We've compiled some techniques here to give you an idea of some of the more common methods. Reality denial manipulation can be quite nasty, so you will want to study these techniques so that you can recognize when dark manipulation is afoot and is pointed at YOU.

Here are some common methods employed in Gas lighting:

1. Lying about friends to isolate you - Dark manipulators want you isolated and, to do that, they need to erode your base of support. They begin dropping hints about your friends, accusing them of belittling you behind your back, not respecting you, or having a romantic interest in the manipulator. They know which buttons to push so this can be very effective, especially if they have been using the next item on our list.

2. They often take their time to become your best friend - Master dark manipulators will take their time to begin tampering with your mental stability. It will likely begin with small examples from this list and then proceed to a full-on assault. Over time, it gets worse and worse and there is added confusion from the 'nice period' that came before. Watch for small examples from this list and, if you see them, take it as a warning sign.

3. Project their feelings on to you - Dark manipulators will often project their feelings and insecurities to you. A very common example in a relationship with one of these individuals is constant accusations that you might be cheating on them. You'll notice that they seem to know a lot about the subject, and this is a warning sign that can help you see what is going on more quickly. If you are getting accusations of this sort for no reason, then be on the alert and ask yourself why they seem to know so much about how a cheating person is likely to act.

4. Tell you that you are imagining things - This generally goes with the previous relationship tactic and can be indicative that they are doing something or many things behind your back. In relationships, we tend to notice when our partners experience a change in behavior. If it is easier to accuse you of having an overactive imagination than it is to explain themselves so that you don't worry, this can be a very big warning sign to watch.

5. Lie to discredit your memory - This is a favorite Gas lighting tactic and very easy to do. If someone sets up a day to meet, for instance, and then later tells you that they never set that up time to meet with you, then you will find it curious at first, but likely never suspect it to be deliberate. They can also express interest in going to a concert or a movie with you and then, when the time comes, act bored or irritated at the event, later claiming that they told you that they didn't want to go to that but that you insisted. It is a tried and true technique and you should watch out for it. A good way to combat this is simply write things down or put them in your calendar immediately and discretely, so that you will know if it occurs more than once. If so, either their memory is quite poor or they may be attempting to Gas light you.

6. Get you angry and accuse you of being crazy - When a dark manipulator knows how to push your buttons, they will often take advantage of this to make you doubt your very sanity by using your temper. It will seem as if every quarrel consists of you yelling and frustrated, while they calmly suggest you have a drink, relax, or perhaps that you both meet another time 'when you are less irrational' or 'less crazy.' Of course, this will make you angrier, giving them an excuse to leave, and later to question whether or not your response was appropriate (especially if followed by the silent treatment, forcing you to communicate first). If you DO have a temper, that doesn't necessarily mean that someone is taking advantage of it, but a constructive way to help determine what occurred is to write down your version of events when you get home and wait to read it until the next day. That way, you can view it when you are less upset and if it is occurring regularly, you

will be better equipped to determine if it is an actual problem with anger, or if this person might be manipulating you towards their ends.

7. Mix abuse with praise or gifts - Dark manipulators like to keep you off-balance by mixing abuse with praise. For instance, you may find yourself being complimented for something innocuous after a brutal argument, or treated to a nice dinner or event after days of silence, with the abusive behavior which was recently experienced never spoke of... as if it never happened. These mixed messages allow the manipulator to prolong their control. If someone is being abusive in the first place, it is best to disassociate with them as soon as possible but, barring this, analyze their behavior and look for patterns from this list.

8. They will use your children - If you have children, dark manipulators will not hesitate to use them against you – raising the volume of their speech so that you will capitulate with their wishes, rather than let your children hear you arguing. They will also bribe children with treats and push your buttons so children will always associate the manipulator with ice cream and toys and anger and yelling. If you notice this behavior, take it for exactly what it is, blatant manipulation, and get as far away as you can from this individual. This is not the sort of thing that gets better over time.

9. Accuse you of wasting efforts in the wrong place – This one can occur in the home or the workplace. You will find your Manager asking, "Why are you wasting time doing this particular assignment when I needed you to do this other one?" after asking you to focus on the first. This is an attempt to bully you, an act of dominance. The only way to combat this is to mark items on your calendar 'Priority per Boss' as they come in or, otherwise, create a paper trail for yourself. While taxing and monotonous, this method is an effective way to defend yourself from manipulation.

10. Turn others against you - Gas lighters know the people who dislike you already and will resort to name dropping to this effect. "Joe knows you are lazy at work" or "Jill says you cheated on a boyfriend once." This

works well with the isolation technique as suddenly not only do you not have your friends, but everyone around is an enemy. Watch out for name-dropping of this sort, as dark manipulators love to use this technique.

We hope that this list of techniques employed by dark manipulators has been of use to you. Use this information well and you'll certainly have the basics of defense at hand should you need it!

Chapter 13: How to Avoid Being Gaslighted

Education. The first step to avoiding being gaslighted is education. Being able to spot the tell-tale signs of gaslighting can be a deciding factor in whether you'll become a victim. Many people become victims of gaslighting because they do not know how gaslighters operate. They spend most of their time thinking that they are the problem, so the gaslighter just continues abusing them. It is a good thing that you are educating yourself on gaslighting by reading this book. And by now, I believe you know the modus operandi of gaslighters. So, when next you encounter a narcissist or a gaslighter, and they try to pull a fast one on you, quickly remind yourself that you are not the problem—they are the problem.

One trick you can use to remind yourself that the gaslighter is the problem is to understand that they are probably doing it because they are trying to remedy their low self-esteem, or perhaps it is because they're trying to regain control of their own lives. Once you convince yourself that they are acting the way they do because of their battles, you will learn to consider their treatments lightly, which means more control. Now that you are not taking them seriously, you are regaining the power you were being denied in the relationship.

The ability to understand that they are the problem and not you will help you regain control of your life and position. It will also be easier not to take what they say personally, thus thwarting their plans and goals to manipulate you.

Get outside advice. Gaslighters aim to have you not trust your mind. If you cannot judge your position, feelings, or reasoning, get someone you trust to help you assess the situation. This step is important early on, as a gaslighter might try to make you distrust those people. But you must learn to get outside advice because if you only listen to your gaslighter, they will confuse you even further. The way out is meant to help you keep your external relationships as strong as possible. It is even possible for your friends and families to notice something off and help you so that you don't get swallowed up by the abuse.

In terms of your external relationships, if you break off from a gaslighter in the process of avoiding gaslighting, you may need a sturdy support system (outside relationships); this is especially crucial if the gaslighter is your partner. If you do not have this support system in place, the gaslighter might maneuver their way back into your life.

Remove yourself from the situation. At work, if you are unable to change positions or companies, you can have HR assess the situation and help you work out a way in which you will not have to work with the gaslighter. This may lead to the abuser switching to another target if they find a suitable one. Spreading information on gaslighting around can be helpful to others as well.

In the family, it may be more difficult. You can move (even to a different city) if you can do so. Try to cut off all contact with the gaslighter. In relationships, it's vital to recognize the symptoms early on. Otherwise, you may get pulled into the abuser's scheme. End a relationship with a gaslighter as soon as possible.

Sometimes, it might not be easy for you to just walk out on the abuser like when they are a co-worker, and you cannot easily change jobs.

Change Your Perspective

Shift your perspective from being a victim to being a winner, warrior, or whatever word feels the most empowering to you. You don't have to keep on being a victim for the rest of your life, and by retrieving your power, you'll also be able to help others in similar circumstances.

Ignore Motives

Most gaslighters have a motive for their gaslighting, and more often than not, it is to control you. There could be other reasons we saw in the film Gaslight where Gregory's motive was to steal Paula's inheritance. But you must ignore the motives. If you don't, you will be further trapping yourself because it will never be apparent, and it will increase your confusion and self-doubt.

Using Cognitive Behavioral Therapy To Avoid Gaslighting

As you already know, gaslighting thrives on your perception of yourself. While the methods and steps can help you avoid gaslighting, it may be difficult for you alone to handle, especially if the gaslighter has firmly wrapped their hands around your mind. Cognitive-behavioral therapy (CBT) is a type of therapy that is concerned with your perception of yourself. It looks at the impact of your thoughts on your behavior. It is also effective for other mental health issues such as anxiety and depression.

For us to see just how CBT can help you avoid gaslighting, let's look at the ABC's of gaslighting. The ABC's stand for Activating, Belief, and Consequences. Activating is the issue that triggers the belief that brings about the consequences. In the case of gaslighting, the gaslighter's attitude towards you is the activating. This activating is not the cause of your trauma; it is the thought or interpretation you give to it that brings about the consequences, which is the trauma. So, if you interpret the gaslighter's actions to mean that your instincts are not correct and you are insane, then the trauma sets in. But if you refuse to interpret it that way, then you will save yourself from the impending trauma. CBT says that if you allow yourself to accommodate negative thoughts always, then it will weigh you down. That is why you can use CBT not to feel what the gaslighter wants you to feel.

Another reason why CBT can help you avoid gaslighting is that a therapist uses structured sessions to become aware of the lies and deceit around you. If you become more aware of the situation around you, then it is very unlikely that you will allow it to get to you.

CBT is a therapy that will require a therapist to carry out effectively. So, you might need to contact a therapist to help you avoid becoming a gaslighting victim or falling back into old habits.

Lightning Source UK Ltd.
Milton Keynes UK
UKHW021936180822
407522UK00003B/122